A Welcome from the Dean

Welcome to Exeter Cathedral!

From the outside, the building has a distinctive shape. The west front, with its wonderful window and its weather-battered screen running across, doesn't soar upwards. The main part of the cathedral seems to be wedged between the two massive and majestic Norman towers. You cannot guess what you will find inside.

The cathedral seems bigger inside than out. Inside, everything is light and spacious. It's on a human, welcoming scale, but at the same time is surprisingly grand, with the arches making a vista of branching stone into the distance.

All the details are perfect, and they all come together in one design. The centuries have been rough with the outside, but inside much ancient carving and painting has survived. And today the cathedral is still used for the same purpose for which it was built. Every day the round of prayers goes on, almost unbroken through the years. And just as the Bishops who built the cathedral wanted it to be filled with music, so it is today.

Make your visit slowly. Notice the details everywhere. In this building is gathered much of the history of this part of England, its famous old families and its ordinary people, the clergy who have worked here and the soldiers and sailors of Devon who have served and died around the world. When you visit, you are part of it as well. You may want to leave a prayer, or light a candle, or just sit and enjoy being here.

I hope you will remember Exeter Cathedral as a place where you have found holiness and peace. And that the memory will please you and refresh you. May God bless you.

The cathedral stands where the Second Augusta Legion of the Roman emperor Vespasian built a fortress. Excavation on the west front uncovered the legion's bathhouse, now under the processional steps. The Roman name for the town that later grew within the defences was *Isca Dumnoniorum*; the Saxons called it *Isca Chester*, later corrupted to Exeter.

Pottery from the 4th century bearing the Chi Ro sign, found nearby, attests to early Christian worship here. Excavation also revealed the site of a Saxon minster where, documents record, a certain Wynfrith was trained *c.*680. Later, known as Boniface, he converted the Saxons of the Rhineland and became the first Bishop of Mainz; he is considered the first apostle of Germany.

In the 9th century, the city was twice taken by the Danes and twice recaptured by the English. In 931 it was occupied by King Alfred's grandson, Athelstan. A late record says that he drove the British out of Exeter and set up the boundary on the Tamar! Athelstan established a new minster, destroyed in 1003 by the Danish king Sweyn. It was repaired as an act of piety by Sweyn's son, Canute, in 1019.

RIGHT: A Saxon tomb in the Lady Chapel, said to be that of Leofric, first Bishop of Exeter. ⑱

ABOVE: King Edward the Confessor, who founded the Diocese of Exeter in 1050. A detail from the west window by Bell & Bell. ①

In this building King Edward the Confessor installed Leofric as first Bishop of Exeter (covering Devon and Cornwall) in 1050. His diploma, to which he and many ecclesiastical and lay magnates subscribed, is in the cathedral archive. Leofric reordered the community into a foundation of 24 canons to lead a life of

The east end and south tower of the cathedral, viewed from the gardens of the Bishop's Palace, seen on the left.

communal worship. The present Dean and Chapter have unbroken succession from this foundation. Leofric made gifts of lands and books to the cathedral. Most of the books were acquired by Thomas Bodley (whose brother was a canon of Exeter) to form part of his library (the Bodleian) in Oxford in 1602. The most important book that remains is a 10th-century codex, the Exeter Book, containing a large and varied collection of Old English poetry. It is one of the chief monuments of Anglo-Saxon literature and the foundation artefact of the cathedral library, now of considerable size and importance and housed in the Bishop's Palace. Also in the library is the Exon Domesday, William the Conqueror's survey of lands and holdings of the five south-western counties, used in the compilation of the great Domesday book of 1086.

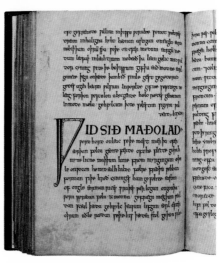

ABOVE: *A detail from the 10th-century Exeter Book in the cathedral library.*

3

In 1107 William the Conqueror's nephew, William Warelwast, became Bishop of Exeter, and seven years later set about the building of a new cathedral in the Romanesque style of the time. This was dedicated in 1133 though work was not completed until about 1180. It was damaged in the siege of Exeter by King Stephen in 1136 and the King paid handsome damages for its repair. The twin towers and the lower parts of the nave walls remain from this church.

Additions were made in the 13th century. Bishop Brewer had a Chapter House built in his garden, adjoining the cathedral, and a cloistered walk to connect to it. Unfortunately the Chapter House was burnt down to the lower walls at the beginning of the 15th century and had to be rebuilt. The fine hammer-beam roof is of this period. The cloister was completed by Bishop Grandisson in the 14th century but was demolished in 1655 during the Commonwealth of Oliver Cromwell.

Today, cathedrals of ancient foundation are governed by a chapter of canons led by the Dean as first among equals. In 1225 Bishop Brewer reorganized the government of the cathedral. He appointed Serlo, the Archdeacon of Exeter, to be its first Dean and gave him a Precentor, a Chancellor and a Treasurer to manage the business of the cathedral. The precentor, or first singer, had care of the singing and worship. His deputy or vicar was the succentor or second singer; the chancellor corrected mistakes in the service books (they were written by hand), drafted business letters and gave lectures on theology and canon law; the treasurer had care of the lights, bells, plate, furniture, vestments (the treasures) and security of the cathedral; his deputy or vicar was the sacristan. These four dignities still exist and are referred to in the statutes as the *quattuor personae*, and have stalls at each corner of the quire. There were also two canons called seneschals who had care of the money, while another canon was sub-dean and acted as confessor or 'penitentiary' to the foundation. This establishment has survived, largely in the same form, to the present day.

ABOVE: *The hammer-beam roof of the Chapter House. First built in the 13th century, this ancient administrative centre was destroyed by fire in the early 15th century, and rebuilt almost totally.* ㉕

TROUBLED TIMES

The close around the cathedral was surrounded by walls and gates by Royal permission in 1286 as a result of the sensational quarrels between the city and cathedral authorities which resulted in the murder of the Precentor, Walter de Lechlade, in 1283. When King Edward I held the Christmas feast at Exeter in 1285 he gave judgement on the matter and hanged the Mayor and sundry other laymen and ordered the punishment of numerous clergy.

ABOVE: *A weekly meeting of the Dean, canons and staff.*

OPPOSITE: *The 13th-century bishop's throne. The Greek for throne is* kathedra, *which is how the cathedral, mother church of the Diocese of Exeter, gets its name.* ⑫

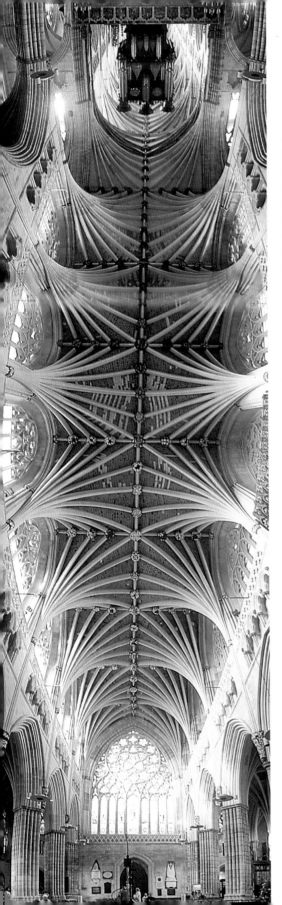

In 1258 the dedication of Salisbury Cathedral, built in the Gothic style, took place. King Henry III and many of his bishops and magnates were in attendance. Most bishops returned to their dioceses determined to have a building in the new style. Bishop Bronescombe of Exeter was no exception. Within 12 years he had raised enough money and had found suitable craftsmen to begin building. It started at the east end of the Norman cathedral with the Lady Chapel and the chapels of St John the Evangelist and St Gabriel. The work was in a development of the Gothic style, known as 'Decorated'. This featured large pairs of windows matching each other across the aisle, and stone ribs rising from the tops of the pillars to meet the central rib of the vault with carved and coloured bosses at the intersections.

As the work progressed westwards, and the new presbytery and quire were built, this stonework became more elaborate, with carved and coloured corbels where ribs met pillars. When the building reached the Norman towers at the crossing the architect conceived a bold plan. Supporting walls and arches were built inside the tower in the new style. Large windows were punched through the north and south walls and the inner walls were taken away. The towers still stand!

The most generous donor to the building was Bishop Stapledon, Treasurer of England for King Edward II and founder of Exeter College, Oxford. He also gave the oak for the Bishop's throne, which was built in 1314. He led an unsuccessful embassy to France concerning the Duchy of Aquitaine and was murdered by a London mob on his return in 1326. The nave was completed in the lifetime of his successor – Bishop Grandisson, who died in 1369 – and included the Minstrels' Gallery and the lower tier of the image screen on the west front. As a former chaplain to the Pope, Grandisson wrote to John XXII describing his new cathedral as 'a church that would rival all the cathedrals of England and France'.

LEFT: A spectacular panoramic view of the quire vault. ⑫

RIGHT: The votive candle holder in the Lady Chapel. Many people find comfort in a lighted candle as an outward and visible expression of their prayers. ⑱

ABOVE: *The Lady Chapel, with its Costessey glass window, was begun in 1270, and dedicated to the Virgin Mary in the medieval fashion. It is now used for daily services.* ⑱

RIGHT: *A statue of the Madonna and Child from the Lady Chapel.* ⑱

In medieval times, a person's ultimate destination – heaven or hell – was a preoccupation of all ranks of society. For the wealthy, one attempted means of avoiding purgatory was the founding of chantries.

The word derives from the 'singing' of a Requiem mass, and a chantry was an altar or chapel endowed by a rich donor. Here special chantry priests would celebrate masses for the soul of their departed benefactor, his relatives and friends.

At Exeter, these priests were known as Annuellars and had their own buildings in the area to the north of the cathedral, where 1–5, The Close now stand. Advocates of Reformation abhorred this practice and funds to provide for it were dissolved by an Act passed in 1547.

LEFT: *A rebus, a pun in stone, of 'Owl-dom' in Bishop Oldham's chantry.* ⑳

The chantries of Precentor Sylke, Sir John Speke and Bishop Hugo (or Hugh) Oldham still survive. Sylke's chantry in the Chapel of the Holy Cross contains a medieval wall-painting of the Resurrection. Speke's chantry (Chapel of St George) has a stone reredos, made by Sir George Gilbert Scott, covering a door made during the Commonwealth (see page 14). Bishop Oldham's chantry (Chapel of St Saviour) is decorated with owls and has a perfect rebus, shown above. Besides founding Manchester Grammar School, Oldham persuaded his friend, Bishop Fox of Winchester, to use the money from the suppression of the alien priories to found a college for the new learning (secular texts in Greek and Latin) and is therefore named as 'co-founder' of Corpus Christi College, Oxford. Oldham lies in a tomb hollowed from the wall because he had been excommunicated following a quarrel with the Bishop of Tavistock.

LEFT: *St George's Chapel, a chantry built by Sir John Speke in 1517. The Gilbert Scott reredos conceals a 17th-century entrance to the cathedral.* ⑮

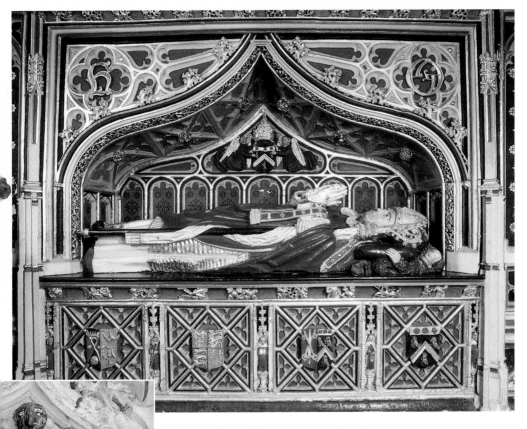

ABOVE: Bishop Oldham, excommunicated for a quarrel with the Bishop of Tavistock, lies in a tomb hollowed in the wall. ⑳

LEFT: The shield of Henry, Marquis of Exeter, 8th Earl of Devon, executed for treason in 1538. ⑮

RIGHT: The Good Shepherd, a bronze by Rosanne Keller in the south quire aisle. ㉑

CATHEDRAL DIMENSIONS

	Metres	Feet
Total Length	117	383
Nave Length	46	150
Nave Width	22	72
Nave Height	21	68
Transept Width	43	140
Tower Height	44	145
Area	2,750 m²	29,600 ft²

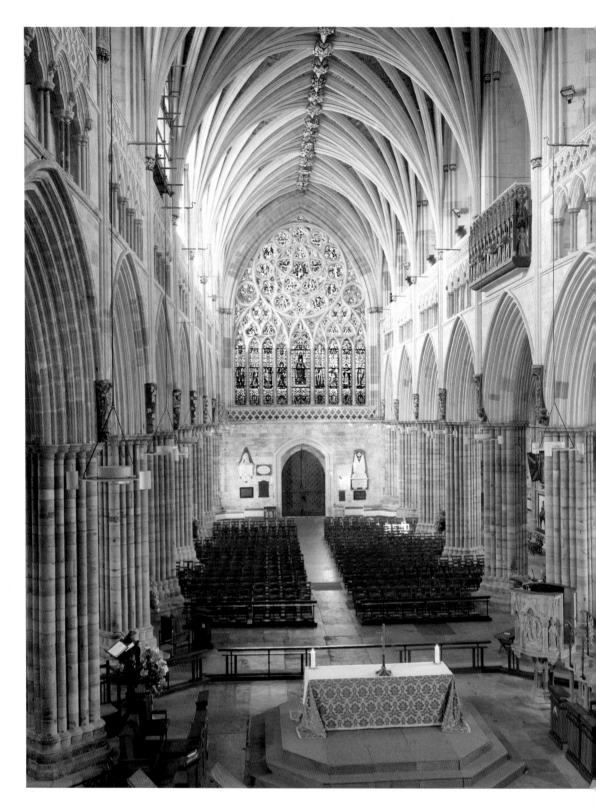

ABOVE: *The nave. The glass of the west window was inserted in 1904, in memory of Frederick Temple, Bishop of Exeter 1869–85 and Archbishop of Canterbury 1896–1902. Destroyed in the Blitz, the window was reglazed in memory of his son, William Temple, born in Exeter and also Archbishop of Canterbury, 1942–44.*

The Tudor times were turbulent for Exeter and the cathedral. Bishop Peter Courtenay had been implicated in the Duke of Buckingham's plot against Richard III and had to flee to France. He returned as part of Henry VII's entourage and was present at the decisive battle of Bosworth in 1485. He donated the clock, to be seen in the north transept, and the 4-ton Peter Bell in the tower above it, on which it still strikes the hours.

Henry VII's grip on the throne was insecure and frequently challenged. When the pretender Perkin Warbeck landed in Cornwall in 1497 and marched towards London he was held up at Exeter, which refused to open its gates. Henry came to the city to administer justice. For its loyalty, he rewarded the city with the gift of the sword of justice and cap of maintenance; Exeter's colours of Tudor green and white date from this time.

Looking down on rebel ringleaders from the Treasurer's house, which then jutted out onto the green from the north tower, Henry dispensed justice. Some were hanged but the majority were pardoned because the King knew the value of clemency.

The reigns of Henry VIII and his children Edward VI, Mary I and Elizabeth I saw great disturbance and change for the Church, as the country experienced 'Reformation'. Because Exeter was of the 'Old Foundation' it was less affected than those cathedrals with monastic orders. These were forced to change to the secular model and are called cathedrals of the 'New Foundation'.

RICHARD HOOKER

On the green, near the Royal Clarence Hotel, is a statue of Richard Hooker. He was born in Exeter, ordained to a Fellowship at Corpus Christi College, Oxford, and died at Sittingbourne, Kent as Rector on 1 November 1600. Hooker wrote a treatise 'Of the Laws of Ecclesiastical Polity', which is one of the greatest works of Anglican theology, providing intellectual justification for Elizabeth I's Church of England.

In 1537 the reformer Simon Heynes was made Dean and began the process of defacing tombs and choir books and destroying the images of saints. Bishop Grandisson's tomb by the west front entrance was destroyed. The changes were not welcomed and in 1549 the people rose against Cranmer's new prayer book, which replaced the Latin rites. The cathedral was beset for about six weeks until the rebels marched on towards London; however they were defeated at Fenny Bridges, east of Honiton. The Vicar of St Thomas, Exeter, was hanged from his own tower for his part in the rising. Further loss occurred in 1552 when the cathedral's plate and jewels were confiscated by the crown.

LEFT: *The clock (c.1485). The sun, shown by a fleur-de-lis, and moon revolve around the earth. The minute dial was added later.* ⑨

THE TUDORS & REFORMATION

The religious fervour that had fuelled the Reformation continued into the 17th century and helped to cause the Civil War. In 1646 Exeter was taken for Parliament by Thomas Fairfax and Oliver Cromwell in command of the Army. The city and cathedral were handed over to a governor, Colonel Hammond. The cathedral was divided into two at the quire screen by a brick wall and a new entrance made to the quire through a door in St George's Chapel. The independents worshipped in the nave under Cromwell's own chaplain, while the Presbyterians worshipped in the quire. Grandisson's cloister was destroyed by a developer in 1655 and a market hall to sell cloth built on the site. The chapter was dispersed and its possessions sequestrated.

The King, Charles II, was restored in 1660 through the intervention of General Monk, a Devon man (and his regiment, the Coldstream Guards, still recruit in the county). The Dean and Chapter returned and their lands were restored. John Loosemore began building an organ in the Chapter House and placed it on the quire screen (or pulpitum) in 1665 where it still stands, though the organ works have been rebuilt several times since.

Exeter also took part in the 'Glorious Revolution' of 1688, when James II was forced into exile. The Prince of Orange, having sailed with a great fleet from Holland to claim his grandfather's throne, held court in the deanery for a week. Sitting in the Bishop's throne in the quire he received the acclamation of the people (while Bishop Lamplugh slipped away), before going on to London to be crowned as William III.

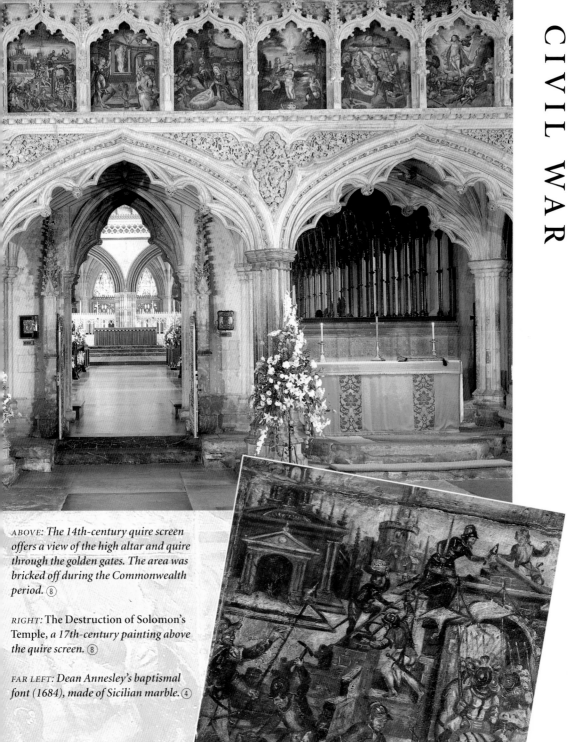

ABOVE: *The 14th-century quire screen offers a view of the high altar and quire through the golden gates. The area was bricked off during the Commonwealth period.* ⑧

RIGHT: The Destruction of Solomon's Temple, *a 17th-century painting above the quire screen.* ⑧

FAR LEFT: *Dean Annesley's baptismal font (1684), made of Sicilian marble.* ④

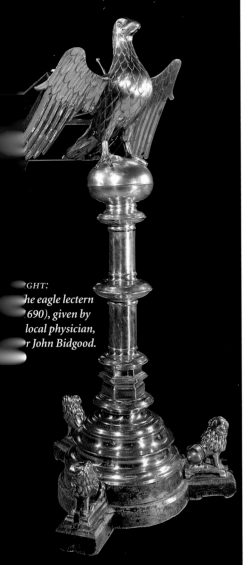

RIGHT:
The eagle lectern
(1690), given by
local physician,
Dr John Bidgood.

After the fervour of the Puritan era and the inter-denominational strife surrounding the Stuart succession came the 'Age of Reason', when religious enthusiasm was unfashionable. The 19th century brought reaction to this. Church affairs once again became a national preoccupation; congregations grew dramatically. This resurgence of interest brought overdue attention to the neglected fabric of many cathedrals, amongst them Exeter.

During the period 1805–1829 a local architect, John Kendall, cleared away many of the crumbling structures attached to the cathedral, including the Treasurer's house and the hovels built along the south wall of the nave, on the site of the cloister, to house six families fallen into poverty during the Commonwealth for their loyalty to the King.

Few English cathedrals failed to call on the services of the architect Sir George Gilbert Scott in the Victorian era. He

ABOVE: *The elephant misericord was carved as early as 1279.* ⑫

began his work at Exeter in 1870 and renovated and refurnished the quire by 1877, the year before his death. His works include the quire stalls, the Martyrs' Pulpit in the nave and the stone reredos in St George's Chapel. In 1887 John Loughborough Pearson, later architect of Truro Cathedral, also set his hand on the fabric with a plan to reconstruct the cloisters. The part he completed now houses the refectory with, above it, the archive. Unfortunately there were insufficient funds to do the whole job and a scheme to use this plan as the Devon war memorial after the First World War also fell through. The memorial cross on the green, designed by yet another famous architect, Sir Edwin Lutyens, is the consolation.

LEFT: *The choir at rehearsal in the impressive setting of the choirstalls.* ⑫

OPPOSITE: *The quire. The organ case was built by John Loosemore in 1665 following the restoration of Charles II. Sir George Gilbert Scott's choirstalls date from his renovation of the quire between 1870 and 1877.* ⑫

The First World War and the effects of the cathedral's loss of lands and properties in the Victorian reforms of 1840 and 1862 left the Dean and Chapter with insufficient funds for the maintenance of the cathedral's fabric and the residential properties in the Close and for support of choral worship. In 1929 the Friends of Exeter Cathedral were formed as a registered charity to help provide the means to keep the cathedral viable. But then another war intervened. On the night of 3–4 May 1942 the German Luftwaffe bombed Exeter for the second time. This was one of the infamous raids on historic cities reputedly chosen from the Baedeker guidebook in revenge for an RAF attack on medieval Lübeck. Much of central Exeter was destroyed.

ABOVE: St Peter protecting the cathedral in the blitz, a window (1957) in the south nave aisle by Christopher Webb.

One bomb hit the cathedral on the south side of the quire destroying the twin Chapel of St James and St Thomas the Martyr, the muniment room above and the organ crypt below, as well as two flying buttresses. The building was shored up and remnants collected. Repair work began in 1947 and the last claim for war damage was paid in 1961. To pay for the extensive repairs, and the maintenance needed to the stonework of the towers and the image screen, the Dean and Chapter had to resort to fresh appeals. The Exeter Cathedral Preservation Trust (a registered charity) is still open and provides resources for the retention of a mason and for structural repairs.

LEFT: The Chapel of St James and St Thomas was destroyed by a bomb in a 'Baedeker' raid on the night of 3 May 1942. ㉒

FAR LEFT: The view from the west door looking east down the nave. The vault measures nearly 100 metres and is the longest true Gothic example in existence. ⑤

The cathedral contains some fine glass of varying antiquity. The oldest is in the great east window which was first constructed at the turn of the 14th century. The earliest lights date from 1304 and show nine figures, amongst them Isaiah, Moses and Abraham; however, the original stone tracery quickly decayed and was replaced in Perpendicular style in 1390. The middle tier of figures of St Sidwell, St Helena, St Edward the Confessor and St Edmund date from this period and were made by Robert Lyen of Exeter in 1391. The glass of the east window was removed and stored during the war so that it did not suffer bomb damage; however, glass from the 18th and 19th centuries was lost in the blitz. The east window was restored in 1948 by Roseveare and again between 1982 and 1986 by Alfred Fisher.

ABOVE AND LEFT: Two details from the east window: the prophet Isaiah, set by Master Walter in 1304, and St Sidwella of Exeter, depicted by the Exeter glazier Robert Lyen in 1391. ⑬

Other medieval glass survives in the clerestory of the quire and in the chapels. The glass of the west window, made as a memorial to Frederick Temple (Bishop of Exeter 1869–85; Archbishop of Canterbury 1896–1902) was blown out in 1942 and has been replaced since the war. Before the Temple memorial this window had been glazed by William Peckitt in 1768. Some surviving lights of his are in the windows of the refectory.

The Lady Chapel contains nine panels of 16th-century French and Flemish glass from the Costessey collection, including the Virgin and Child. The window in the Chapel of St Andrew commemorates the loss of HMS *Exeter*, sunk in the Java Sea on 28 February 1942. St Edmund's Chapel has fine windows of St Michael and St George by Reginald Bell, given by the Devonshire Regiment.

ABOVE: A window by Sir Ninian Comper in the chapel of St Andrew. It is in memory of the crew of HMS Exeter, which was sunk in the Java Sea on 28 February 1942. ⑭

The cathedral contains many monuments and tombs. The oldest is a Bishop's tomb, possibly of Leofric, in the south wall of the Lady Chapel. This chapel also has the fine decorated tombs of Bishops Bronescombe and Stafford. In the presbytery are the highly decorated tombs of Bishop Marshall and Bishop Stapledon. Across the north quire aisle from the Bishop is the canopied tomb of his brother, Sir Richard Stapledon, with his squire and horse beside him (unfortunately beheaded by reformers). Facing one another across the quire are the altar tombs of Bishops Berkeley and Lacy. Both were renowned as healers and their tombs attracted many pilgrims and donations to the cathedral.

The most imposing lay tomb is that of the 2nd Earl of Devon and his countess Margaret de Bohun, in the south transept. Other lay tombs and effigies include Sir Humphrey de Bohun, Earl of Hereford, and Sir Henry de Ralegh in the south quire aisle, Sir John Gilbert of Compton and his wife Elizabeth of Chudleigh in the south transept and of Sir Gawen and Sir Peter Carew in the Chapel of St John the Evangelist.

Canadian visitors may appreciate John Flaxman's monument in the south quire aisle to Lieutenant-General John Simcoe, first governor of Upper Canada (Ontario) with its retainers of a British soldier and an Algonquin Indian.

More recent monuments include the statue in the north transept of James Northcote RA by Sir Francis Chantrey and the monument in the north quire aisle by Marochetti in memory of those 9th Queen's Royal Lancers killed during the Indian Mutiny. R.D. Blackmore, author of the famous Devon novel, *Lorna Doone*, also has a memorial on the wall by the north-west entrance.

LEFT: *An Algonquin Indian guards General Simcoe, first governor of Upper Canada.* ㉑

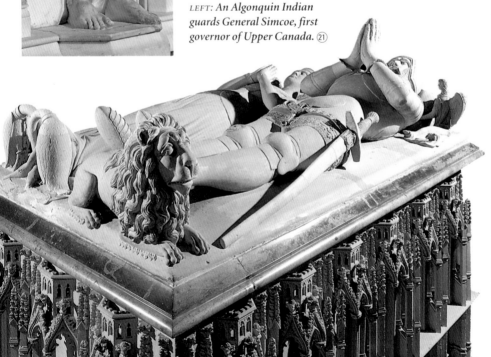

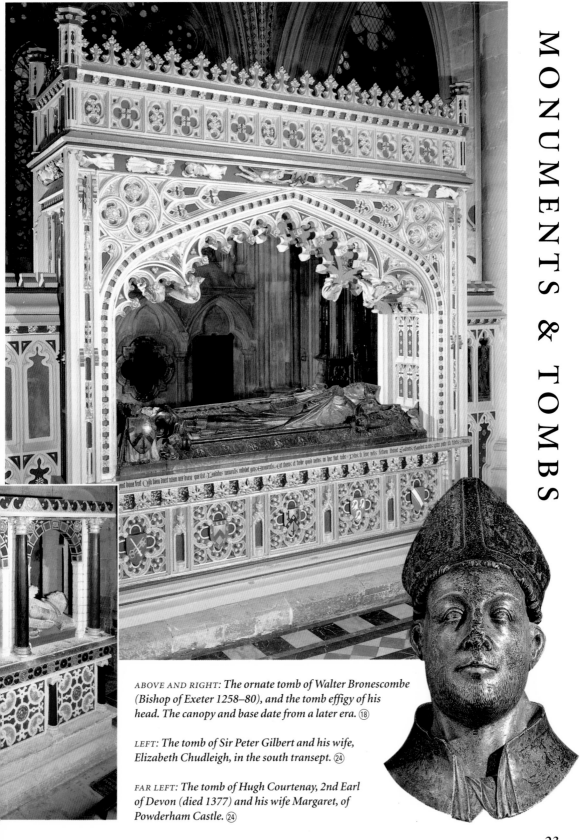

ABOVE AND RIGHT: *The ornate tomb of Walter Bronescombe (Bishop of Exeter 1258–80), and the tomb effigy of his head. The canopy and base date from a later era.* ⑱

LEFT: *The tomb of Sir Peter Gilbert and his wife, Elizabeth Chudleigh, in the south transept.* ㉔

FAR LEFT: *The tomb of Hugh Courtenay, 2nd Earl of Devon (died 1377) and his wife Margaret, of Powderham Castle.* ㉔

ABOVE: Corbel of an acrobatic monk. ⑦

ABOVE: The Becket boss. ⑤

BELOW: St George and the dragon. ⑧

Exeter Cathedral has an unparalleled collection of sculpture from the period 1275–1350. The works demonstrate close observation of nature with naturalistic forms of leaves, animals and humans. Amongst them are several 'Green Men' – an interesting comment on the survival of earlier beliefs amongst the workmen. A fine double-headed Green Man is in the retroquire outside the entrance to the Lady Chapel. More can be seen on corbels, for example, at the north-west end of the quire by the organ case. In the nave, on the north side, above the second pillar from the crossing, is the famous figure of the acrobatic monk, standing on his head and balancing on a violinist. At the other end of the nave and on the south side is a fine corbel depicting the Madonna and Child, standing on a recumbent male.

In the centre of the nave is a boss depicting the murder of Thomas Becket (one of his assailants was from Devon). Another enigmatic boss, almost opposite the Minstrels' Gallery, shows the head of a king. This is sometimes thought to be Edward III, the next boss in the series being his queen, Eleanor, but the shape of the crown is more like the papal diadem so it may represent Bishop Grandisson's old master, Pope John XXII. The Minstrels' Gallery has 14 angels, 12 playing instruments; from west to east these are: citole, bagpipes, recorder, fiddle, harp, missing instrument (possibly a blown brass), short trumpet, portative organ, gittern, shawm, tambourine, cymbals.

The pulpitum (or screen) which divides the quire from the nave was completed in 1324. Above its three depressed ogee arches is a series of panels, once full of sculptures, removed by reformers. These were replaced in the early 17th century with the present paintings. From north to south these depict: the Creation; the birth of Eve from Adam's rib; the Flood; the Red Sea overwhelming Pharaoh and his host; the destruction of Solomon's Temple; the building of the second Temple; the Angel appearing to Zacharias; the birth of Christ; Christ's baptism; Christ being taken down from the Cross; the Resurrection; the descent of the Holy Ghost at Pentecost.

LEFT: The cathedral's finest 'green man'. ⑰

LEFT:
The Minstrels'
Gallery. ⑥

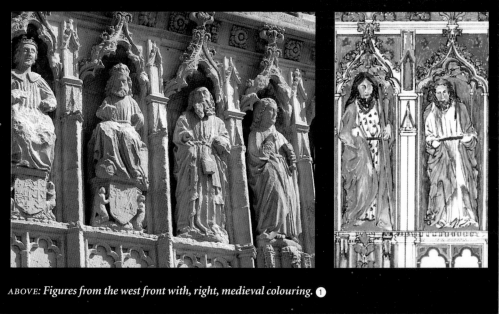

ABOVE: *Figures from the west front with, right, medieval colouring.* ❶

The cathedral's prime purpose is to worship God through Jesus Christ. The Dean and Chapter worship communally whenever possible and Divine Office takes place at least three times each day. Evensong is sung every day except on Wednesday, when it is said. On Sunday the Eucharist is sung as well as mattins, evensong and evening prayer.

This continues a musical tradition going back to the 11th century. Under Bishops Leofric and Grandisson, canons sang the offices, each with a Vicar Choral to sing in his absence. In addition Exeter had 24 boy choristers and some secondaries (older boys transforming from choristers to vicars and receiving education at the Chapter's expense). All singing boys had to play instruments as well as sing polyphonic music.

From the 14th to the 16th centuries the cathedral rang with singing at all hours. There were two high masses, the main one at the high altar and the Lady mass in the Lady Chapel, many low masses and those sung by the chantry priests. In addition there were nine services of Divine Office at the canonical hours. Singing included both plainchant and polyphony.

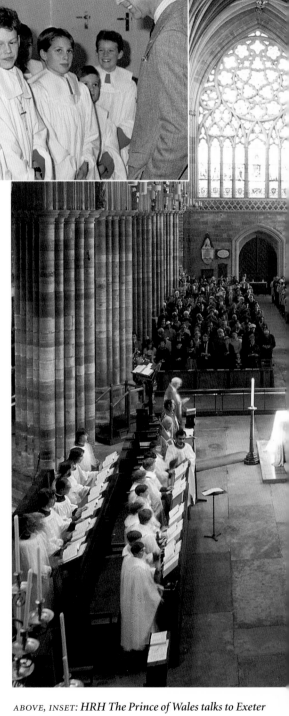

ABOVE: *The administration of bread and wine at the service of Eucharist.*

ABOVE, INSET: *HRH The Prince of Wales talks to Exeter Cathedral choristers.*

ABOVE: *Young musicians rehearse in the nave for a concert. The cathedral is the scene of many exciting musical events during the year.*

LEFT: *A guide and party at the pulpitum. Many thousands of people visit during the year.*

This changed at the Reformation. In 1547 the number of Vicars Choral was reduced to 20, of whom 12 had to be laymen. The number of services was greatly reduced. Nevertheless, the tradition of singing survives. The cathedral's present choir has 14 singing men (lay vicars and choral scholars), 20 boys and 20 girls. There is also a voluntary choir. To maintain the round of services there are daily rehearsals during school terms by the cathedral choir and by visiting choirs at other times.

All choristers attend Exeter Cathedral School, mostly as boarders, and all play instruments as well as sing. It requires as much effort and almost as much money to maintain this part of the cathedral's foundation as it does to maintain the fabric; but without this commitment, the very special sound and art form of English cathedral music would be lost. The Exeter Cathedral Music Foundation Trust and the Friends of Exeter Cathedral both support the continuity of this fine tradition.

ABOVE: *A service of ordination for new priests in the diocese, held in the nave.*

There are many special events on the cathedral calendar. During school holidays, when the bulk of the 400,000 visitors a year come to the cathedral, there are art exhibitions in the Chapter House and in the retroquire, and weekly organ recitals. The nave is used for concerts throughout the year, with many famous orchestras playing, especially during the Exeter Festival in July. At this time there is also the annual craft fair on the green. Other events include annual services for the city and county, for the armed forces and for local universities and schools, as well as carol concerts and dramatic performances.

Keeping the cathedral ready for each event is a heavy duty shared by virgers, office and work staff, guides and stewards, sidesmen, flower arrangers, dusters, embroiderers and bell-ringers. The Fellowship of the cathedral provides refreshments after services and a welcome for visiting parishes, as well as arranging lectures, visits, entertainments and, more seriously, prayer and study groups. Duty chaplains provide a priestly presence in the cathedral throughout the year.

The cathedral and its school have a paid staff of around 100 people, a volunteer force of more than 400 and an annual turnover of £2 million. It is a focal point and vital element in the life of the county of Devon and, like the ancient and loyal city of Exeter, in which it stands, tries always to live up to the motto *Semper Fidelis* – Ever Faithful.

ABOVE: *A mason saws a stone for the south tower restoration.*

LEFT: *How does it stay up? Children experience medieval building techniques at first hand in the cathedral's education department.*